Shakespeare's Globe

The guidebook

SPINNEY PUBLICATIONS

Sam Wanamaker CBE
1919–1993

The new Globe in Southwark is the work of many people and the dream of one man.

When the young American actor came to London in 1949, he set out to visit the site of Shakespeare's Globe and was amazed to find that the only testimony to its existence was a blackened bronze plaque on the wall of a brewery. He conceived of a fitter memorial to the great playwright, a replica of the Globe itself.

Sam Wanamaker's enthusiasm, tenacity and energy inspired a world-wide effort to rebuild the Globe as faithfully as scholarship and craftsmanship could achieve, only a few hundred yards from where Shakespeare's original stood. As you visit the new Globe you are witnessing the fulfilment of Sam's dream.

Shakespeare's Globe

Tribute to Sam Wanamaker

Shakespeare's London   4

Crossing the river   10

The first Globe   14

Setting up the frame   22

Entrances, exits and galleries   28

Thatching the roof   32

The sumptuous stage   36

The Globe Centre   44

Tribute to Theo Crosby

Shakespeare's London

When the Globe was built in 1599, London was a city with growing pains. Its population had doubled in the previous fifty years, to about two hundred thousand inhabitants, and was to double again in the next fifty, making it the biggest city in Europe. That meant huge growth in the suburbs to the north and east and across the river, and pressing problems of control for the Lord Mayor. Policing, along with registering births, deaths and marriages, regulating prices in the local markets and providing relief for the poor, was in the hands of the local parishes, and although the city was for the most part an orderly place, the administrators were always worried, not least by the big crowds drawn to see plays.

The Globe stood on the south bank of the Thames, opposite the city, in the energetic commercial suburb of Southwark. River wherries provided the nearest thing to a taxi service for London, and all heavy goods came in by water. The only way to cross the river on foot was by London Bridge, a medieval, stone-built, many-arched structure. Shops, houses and a chapel were crammed along its length and at either end were large entrance gates where the heads of traitors were displayed. Southwark was full of wayfarers' inns for the many travellers who used London Bridge, including Chaucer's famous Tabard where the pilgrims to Canterbury gathered. The river, its bridge and the nearby streets which were main thoroughfares were always crowded.

Each parish had its own weekly market specialising in its own produce. Southwark's market was in the Borough High Street running south from London Bridge. The parish officers were responsible for regulating everything that went on in the suburb and in the church of St. Mary Overies, which became the parish church of St. Saviours and is now Southwark Cathedral, they kept a record of all their citizens.

opposite Elizabethan gentry being ferried to the south bank. London Bridge, seen in the distance, was, at this time, the only bridge across the Thames.
Michael Van Meer. By permission of Edinburgh University Library La. III 283 fol. 408v.

above Wherries carry passengers on the Thames, past coal barges moored in front of the Tower of London. Transport by river, especially of bulk materials, was normal in 1599.
Wenceslaus Hollar. By permission of Guildhall Library, Corporation of London.

One of them was William Shakespeare's youngest brother Edmund, who followed William to London hoping to become an actor like his rich brother. Edmund, sixteen years younger than William, lived near the Globe. The parish records include an entry registering the birth of his illegitimate son to a local woman. He died in 1607 at the age of only 27, and was buried on the morning of New Year's Eve. Burial services were normally held in the afternoons, at a cost nearer two shillings than the twenty recorded for Edmund's burial. Paying extra to have the service early in the day made it possible for his fellow-actors to attend. They had their plays to perform in the afternoon.

London's Lord Mayors, who controlled every section inside the city walls except for the precinct of St. Paul's and some 'liberties' such as the Blackfriars and parts of Southwark, hated plays. Plays took apprentices and workmen away from their jobs, since they were performed in daylight each afternoon, and they were thought to be profane and ungodly. The Privy Council protected them on the grounds that the Queen enjoyed being entertained by plays at Christmas and needed well-practised players on hand. But for nearly twenty years, through the 1580s and 1590s, the Mayors were trying to have plays banned. So the companies began to move outside the city walls, to suburbs like Shoreditch in the north and Southwark in the south where the Lord Mayor's authority stopped.

The Lord Chamberlain and his son-in-law, the Lord Admiral, set up two new companies in 1594 under their own names. The first company, the Lord Chamberlain's Men, played at the Theatre, north of the city in Shoreditch. This was the company which Shakespeare joined. The other company, the Lord Admiral's, occupied the Rose on Bankside in Southwark. The Rose company had Marlowe's plays,

left An alderman of Southwark in his regalia in 1598.
Hugh Alley. By permission of The Folger Shakespeare Library.

while the Theatre's company had Shakespeare as an actor, along with all his plays. In time Shakespeare's company became the best and the richest of all the companies. It ran continuously for another forty-eight years, until the Civil War began in 1642 and all the theatres were closed.

The ability to pay money and see a professional company performing a play was still quite a new feature of life in London when Shakespeare arrived there from Stratford-upon-Avon sometime in the 1580s. The only other form of professional entertainment routinely on offer was animal-baiting. It had been possible for some years before the first theatres were built in the 1570s to see bulls and bears baited in the arenas on Bankside. The first playhouses resembled the bear and bull-baiting rings. At the new playhouses, three or more companies would perform every afternoon, so long as the epidemics of bubonic plague which recurred most summers did not force the Privy Council to ban public assemblies in London. Despite the hostility of the Lord Mayor and Guildhall, thousands of people went to the new theatres to see plays every day.

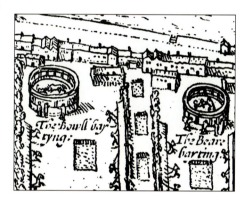

left The Southwark bull and bear-baiting rings on the Bankside in the 1570s.
Braun and Hogenberg. By permission of Guildhall Library, Corporation of London.

below The Southwark market in 1598, showing the stalls of the county merchants in their named spaces. On the left is the market hall where goods were weighed, and a bell was rung to close the market. The faces of offenders can be seen inside the pillory.
Hugh Alley. By permission of The Folger Shakespeare Library.

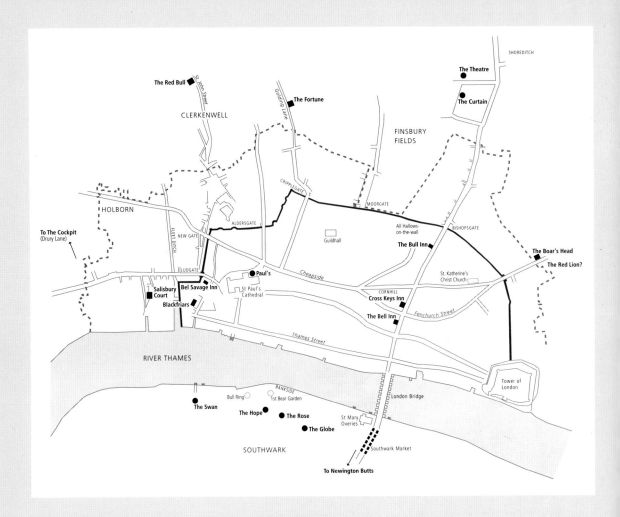

The ten open-air amphitheatres of Shakespeare's time, their locations and their dates:

1576: The Theatre, Finsbury Fields, Shoreditch.

1576: Newington Butts, Southwark, Surrey.

1577: The Curtain, Finsbury Fields, Shoreditch.

1587: The Rose, Bankside, Surrey.

1595: The Swan, Paris Garden, Surrey.

1599: The Globe, Bankside, Surrey.

1600: The Fortune, Golding Lane, Clerkenwell.

1600: The Boar's Head, Whitechapel.

1604: The Red Bull, Clerkenwell.

1614: The Hope (the Bear Garden), Bankside, Surrey.

The five hall playhouses of Shakespeare's time, their locations and their dates:

1576: Paul's, Cathedral precinct.

1576: The (first) Blackfriars, Blackfriars.

1596: The (second) Blackfriars, Blackfriars.

1616: The Cockpit, Drury Lane, Westminster.

1629: The Salisbury Court, Whitefriars.

City inns used for plays between 1576 and 1594, either in yards or indoors:

Bel Savage, Bull, Bell, Cross Keys.

— City walls

⋯ Boundary of area within jurisdiction of Guildhall

■● Halls and other buildings used as theatres

□ Other buildings

above A map of early London and its theatres.

opposite St. Mary Overies (now Southwark Cathedral) in 1616. The heads of traitors are displayed above the entrance gates of London Bridge.
Cornelius Visscher. By permission of Guildhall Library, Corporation of London.

Crossing the river

Early Elizabethan companies acted in inns and inn-yards. It was not until 1576 that the first purpose-built playhouse was set up by the actor-manager James Burbage. He called it the Theatre, establishing the name by which playhouses (the Elizabethan word) are known to this day. With a businessman's eye for profits, Burbage leased a site for his Theatre on a busy main road running north out of the City, just beyond the Lord Mayor's reach.

When Shakespeare came to London from Stratford-on-Avon in the 1580s, he joined the company at the Theatre. For twenty years the Theatre prospered, but in 1596 the landlord Giles Allen refused to renew the lease. James Burbage had to look for a new playhouse. Instead of choosing to build another open-air one, like the Theatre, he fitted out a small theatre in a hall in the Blackfriars below St. Paul's. His intention must have been to move the actors indoors.

The rich inhabitants of the Blackfriars had other ideas. In November 1596 they blocked the company from staging any plays there. They petitioned the Privy Council, saying they did not want a playhouse in their neighbourhood, with its noise and its crowds. *'A generall inconvenience to all the inhabitants ... by reason of the great gathering togeather ... of all manner of vagrant and lewde persons that ... will come thither and worke all manner of mischeefe.'*

James Burbage died in February 1597. Two months later the lease of the Theatre expired. For the next two years his sons Cuthbert and Richard struggled with Giles Allen

opposite Thatch being applied to the roof of the new Globe, across the river from St Paul's. This is the first thatched roof in London since the great fire of 1666.

below John Norden's engraving of 1600. It shows the Swan on the left, and the Rose (misnamed the 'Stare') and the Globe on either side of Maiden Lane, now called Park Street.
By permission of the Royal Library, Stockholm, De la Gardie Collection.

opposite *A Fête at Bermondsey*, by Joris Hoefnagel (1542–1600). The painting shows a stretch of the Thames, with the Tower of London visible across the river. The rural nature of the south bank and its location, close to the City but beyond the Lord Mayor's jurisdiction, made it a popular place for sport and festivities.

By permission of Hatfield House, Hertfordshire/Bridgeman Art Library, London

to renew the lease while the company performed in a rented playhouse, the Curtain. At Christmas 1598 they gave up. They leased a plot of land across the river in Southwark, barely fifty yards from the Rose, the playhouse of their great rivals. They hired a master carpenter, Peter Street, to demolish the Theatre and transport its framing timbers across the Thames to the new site on Bankside. There, in the early months of 1599, he built the first Globe, using whatever he could rescue from the old Theatre.

When he heard of the demolition, Allen promptly sued Street for trespass, claiming that he had taken a massive quantity of building materials from the property. He took Burbage's sons to court where he accused them of theft and of being *'riotous persons'*. The case was still running nearly three years later. It finally died of exhaustion in 1602, leaving the Globe to be *'the glory of the Banke'*.

For fourteen years Shakespeare's company prospered in their *'house with the thatched roof'* until disaster struck again in 1613. During a performance of *Henry VIII* a piece of wadding fired from a stage cannon lodged in the roof, smouldering until the thatch burst into flames and burned the Globe to the ground. The whole audience, perhaps as many as three thousand, left safely by two exit doors, apart from one unfortunate man. *'Certain cannons being shot off,'* wrote Sir Henry Wotton, *'some of the paper or other stuff wherewith one of them was stopped, did light on the Thatch, where being thought at first but an idle smoak, and their Eyes more attentive to the show, it kindled inwardly, and ran round like a train, consuming within less than an hour the whole house to the very ground ... wherein yet nothing did perish but wood and straw, and a few forsaken cloaks, only one man had his breeches set on fire, that would perhaps have broiled him, if he had not, by the benefit of a provident wit, put it out with bottle ale.'*

A thatched roof was a cheap roof in Elizabethan times. When the company re-built their lavish second Globe on the foundations of their burned first Globe, they made sure they gave it a tiled roof. However, when they crossed the river in 1599, Burbage's sons needed to make economies. This was because everything that they had inherited from their father was trapped in the new, but unusable, Blackfriars theatre. They got some money from renting it in 1599 to a new company of boy players who were less objectionable to the rich residents of the Blackfriars liberty. It was not, however, enough to pay for building the Globe.

This led to a new deal, which accidentally secured the future of the company. The Burbages offered other leading players shares in the new building and Shakespeare was one of four who joined the syndicate. Thus he came to be the owner of one-eighth of the Globe, the playhouse for which he wrote his greatest plays.

right Richard Burbage, leading actor and part-sharer in the company of the Lord Chamberlain's Men.
By permission of the Trustees of Dulwich Picture Gallery

CROSSING THE RIVER

The first Globe

left The remains of the Globe, uncovered in 1989, with an archaeologist's diagram offering a possible interpretation.
Graphic by Museum of London Archæology Service.© Museum of London.
Photograph by Museum of London Archæology Service.© Museum of London.

below Hazelnut shells were found in the remains of the Globe. It is thought that they were used as part of a composite mixture covering the floor of the yard.
© The University of Reading Photographic Unit.

How do we know what the first Globe looked like? Happily, a lot of evidence exists. Although much is circumstantial, there are sufficient clues to be certain of many aspects of the Globe's construction and appearance.

On contemporary engravings of London, the Globe and the Rose stand out, landmarks of the south bank. Sketches and prints of the interiors of theatres also survive, most famously one by the Dutchman De Witt of the inside of the Swan. Three years before the Globe was built De Witt visited London, and he took note of four playhouses, two of them south of the river. *'There are four amphitheatres in London of notable beauty … In each of them a different play is daily exhibited to the populace. The two more magnificent of these are situated to the south beyond the Thames and are called the Rose and the Swan.'* Thomas Platter, visiting from Basle in 1599, was able to see a performance at the newly-built Globe. *'On September 21st after lunch, about two o'clock, I and my party crossed the water, and there in the house with the thatched roof witnessed an excellent performance of the tragedy of the first Emperor Julius Cæsar.'*

The most tangible evidence we have is archaeological. In January 1989 archaeologists working on a redevelopment site east of Rose Alley and north of Park Street

uncovered the remains of the Rose Theatre. About three-fifths of the original foundations were evaluated. This confirmed what scholars had long believed, that Elizabethan open-air playhouses were many-sided buildings. The Rose foundations now lie under a new office block, carefully preserved and monitored.

Encouraged by this fortunate discovery, Museum of London archæologists tried to locate the Globe, and in October of the same year they uncovered about 5% of its foundations. They were able to evaluate though not excavate them. Part of the Globe is buried under Southwark Bridge Road; most lies beneath Anchor Terrace, a nineteenth-century listed building. Exactly what part of the theatre the foundations represent is still unclear, but the fragments helped scholars to predict the shape and dimensions of the Globe. Who knows what future discoveries will reveal?

The Chorus in *Henry V* describes the Globe as a hollow circle, appealing to the spectators to use their imaginations to fill the playhouse with the armies of France and England, to

cram
Within this wooden O the very casques
That did affright the air at Agincourt.

One solitary engraving of the first Globe by John Norden survives. Blotchy and minimalist though it is, it appears to show a round building. So also does Wenceslaus Hollar's fine engraving of the second Globe which was built on the foundations of the first.

Elizabethan playhouses were not shaped like doughnuts, however round they looked from a distance. Wood does not lend itself easily to circular constructions, and the frame of the Globe needed to be both strong and stable to support three tiers of galleries. A succession of straight-sided timber bays, jointed

above left A detail from John Norden's 1600 engraving of the Globe and the Rose (misnamed the 'Stare'). The remains of the two rival theatres still lie close by each other, on either side of Park Street and Southwark Bridge Road.
By permission of the Royal Library, Stockholm, De la Gardie Collection.

above Tudor bricks were slimmer than modern ones. To build the foundation wall of the new Globe, bricks had to be specially made to the Elizabethan measurements.
© Pentagram Design Limited.

right The foundations of the Rose theatre, discovered in 1989. In spite of the intrusive groups of round, concrete pillars, (the remains of a 1950s building demolished in 1988), the outline of the Rose's stage and the polygonal shape of the galleries are clear.
© Andrew Fulgoni Photography / Museum of London

THE FIRST GLOBE

right The second Globe was drawn by Wenceslaus Hollar in the 1630s. He stood on the tower of St Mary Overies and traced an accurate outline of what he saw, using a topographical glass. This drawing was the basis of his famous engraving, the 'Long View of London', 1647. Hollar's drawing, confirmed by archæology, provided scholarly evidence for the shape of the Globe.
By permission of the Yale Center for British Art, Paul Mellon Collection.

below Architectural diagrams of the new Globe.
© Pentagram Design Limited.

together into a polygon, is the practical way to build a circular shape in wood. The crucial question was – how many sides did it take to complete the circle?

For many years guesses at the Globe's dimensions ranged from 16 to 24 sides with a width of 80 to 100 feet. Almost at the last moment, the discovery of the foundations of the original changed all this. Scholars deduced from the 162 degree angle between the wall fragments of two bays that Shakespeare's Globe had twenty sides and a diameter of 100 feet. The new Globe is built to these measurements.

Ben Jonson wrote of the first Globe that it was *'Flanck'd with a ditch, and forc'd out of a Marish'*. Southwark was a marshy place in Elizabethan times. The tidal Thames in the section upriver of London Bridge where the playhouses were built would flood occasionally. The first problem any builder had to face was drainage.

The foundations of the Globe were made by digging trenches in the outline of the inner and outer gallery walls. These trenches were filled with stone, mainly lumps of limestone from the Thames estuary, known as 'clunch'. On top of the stone foundations, brick walls were built, wide enough to hold oak groundsills, the horizontal base beams of the giant timber frame, and high enough to lift the frame out of the damp ground. Bedded in lime mortar, with the grain laid horizontally along the brick walls,

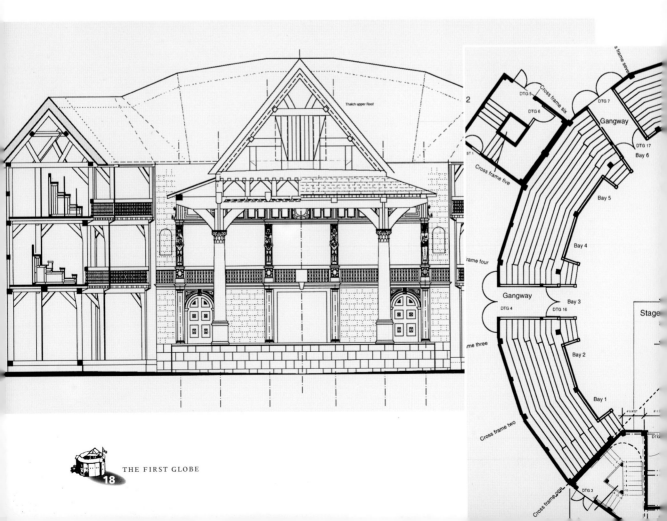

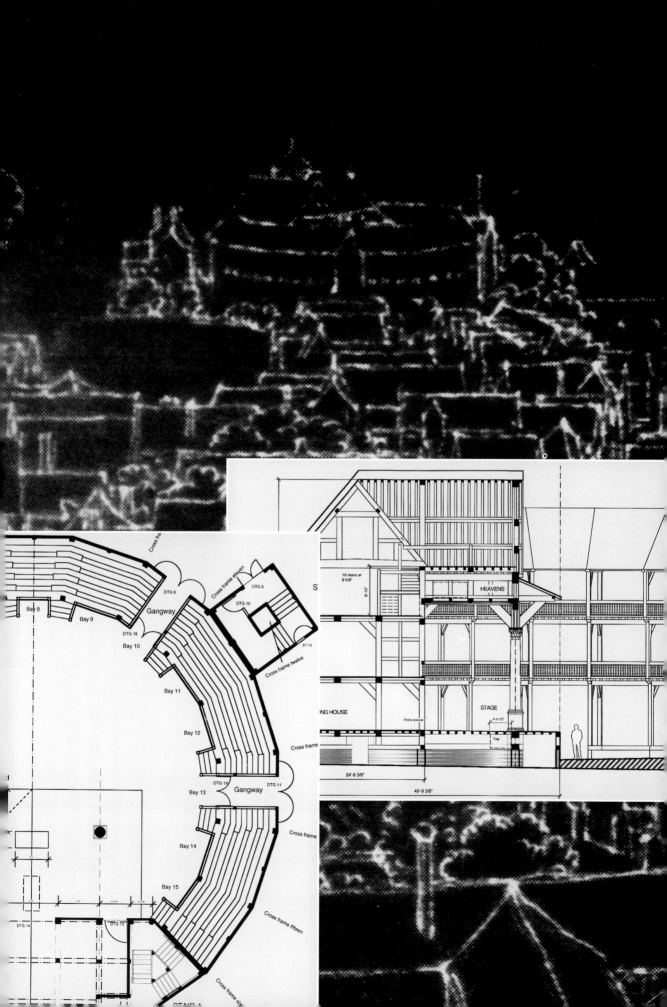

the oak groundsills act as a barrier against rising damp.

As with the original, so with the new Globe: before work could start on the theatre the site had to be secured against the Thames. A diaphragm wall was sunk below ground level, 300 metres long, 20 metres high and 0.6 metres thick. Over this lies a concrete piazza on which the new Globe stands, slightly higher than the original, looking across the river to St. Paul's. Little of the underpinning is visible, but the space created beneath the piazza will house the Globe's exhibitions. In the undercroft directly beneath the theatre are buried the Time Capsules, stainless-steel containers filled with a collection of objects from the 1990s by the schools who raised money for the Globe's Heavens.

In a shape that looks from above like a funnel designed to catch rainwater, good drainage mattered. In wet weather, the thatch on the gallery roof dripped. In *The Tempest* Ariel says of the weeping Gonzalo

His tears run down his beard like
   winter's drops
From eaves of reeds.

Ditches outside the theatre channelled the rainwater away, probably north to the Thames. Inside, if the Globe followed the design indicated by the Rose excavations, the yard would have sloped quite steeply towards the centre where a barrel was sunk to catch rainwater. Beneath the mortared surface of the yard, drainage pipes ran out from the barrel. These would have been wooden pipes made from long tree-trunks hollowed out with a pump auger.

The unexpected discovery at the Rose was that on top of the mortared yard surface a second, flatter surface had been applied. This was a mixture of hazelnut shells, cinders, ash, sand and silt. The same surfacing was found when a small part of the Globe was excavated. At first it was assumed that the hazelnut shells had been discarded by nut-chewing spectators: Elizabethan 'popcorn', the press dubbed them.

The archæologists were more cautious. The mixture of ash and shells was so uniform throughout that they felt it must have been an intentional part of the construction. Recent scholarship points to the local soapworks as the likely source because soap boilers, after extracting oil from nuts and lye from wood-ash to make soap, discarded the shells and ashes as freely available 'industrial waste'. The yard of the new Globe has been given a mortar undersurface, sloping like the yard surface of the Rose, and tarred with a waterproof sealant. Over this is a deep layer of the same mix of ash, clinker, sand and hazel-nut shells that the archæologists found covering the yards of the Rose and the Globe.

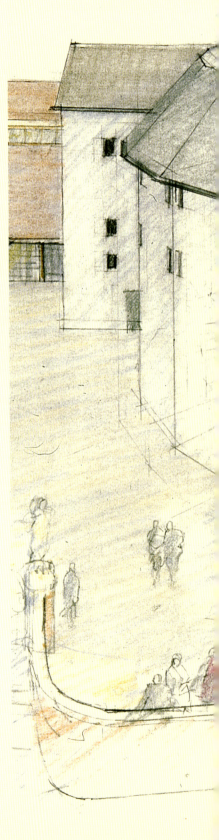

right A sketch by Dennis Bailey of an early version of the new Globe. The stage cover was altered in the final design and an extra 'skirt' or pentice roof was added.
© Dennis Bailey, Pentagram Design Limited.

above The groundsills are laid out in the workshop.
© Peter McCurdy.

right Joints are cut using a tool called a 'slick'.
© Peter McCurdy.

Setting up the frame

From the low, brick plinth wall running round the foundation trenches, twenty huge oak timbers rise 32 feet into the air to form the main frame of the new Globe. In 1599 Street had to re-use the seasoned timbers taken from the Theatre after the lease ran out. Getting the pegs out of the hardened joints without splitting the wood cannot have been easy. Oak from a freshly-cut tree is much easier to work than wood which has weathered. No timber is perfectly straight. Each beam has to be individually cut and marked for assembly into its own unique place in the structure. Street must have re-assembled the frame of the first Globe carefully and with difficulty, closely following the pattern of the dismantled Theatre.

Street was able to use green oak the following year when he built his second playhouse, the Fortune. Unlike his work on the Globe, documentary evidence about how he constructed it has survived. He took twelve workmen into the forest by the Thames at Sonning and spent the next three months getting teams of sawyers to cut down trees he chose, and hew and rough-cut them in their sawpits into the basic

left The master craftsman selects a tree.
© Peter McCurdy.

below The marked tenon is ready to slot into its unique mortice.
© Peter McCurdy.

Photograph Richard Kalina

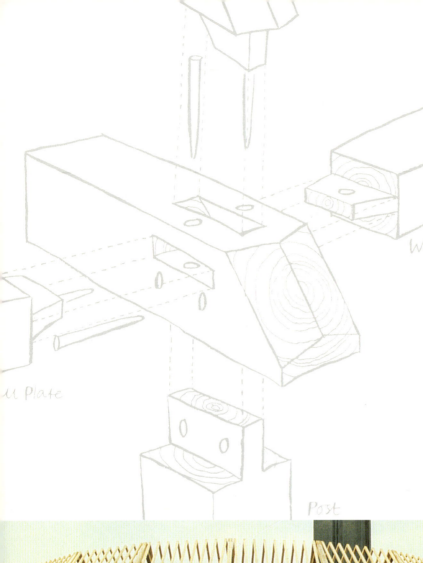

shapes he wanted. His workmen made the building frame, trimming the logs with axes and cutting mortice and tenon joints to fit them together. Each bay of the frame was laid out flat on the ground in a clearing in the forest, each mortice and tenon joint given a distinctive mark before the beams were dismantled and carted off for re-erection in London.

In the 1990s the same traditional techniques have been used to build the new Globe. Every bay is made of a number of frames and many timbers. Each timber was marked, jointed and shaped. The frames were assembled flat on the floor of Peter McCurdy's workshop near Newbury before being disassembled and transported to Bankside where

they were re-assembled, bay by bay. As the skeletal frame began to rise beside the Thames, Londoners might have wondered whether a building was going up or coming down.

Most of the joints are mortice and tenon, fixed with tapered wooden pegs. Over 6,000 of them are driven into holes slightly off-set. The narrow end of the peg slips easily into the part where the two holes overlap but as the peg widens it draws the holes into line with each other, tightening the timber joint.

Once the bays were set up on site, the infilling of the walls began. Oak staves, substantial secondary timbers, were fitted vertically into the panels of the frames and across these were nailed thin laths, cleft from oak. Through the narrow gaps in the laths, plaster was stuffed to fill the cavities and then built up in a series of coats, the last one smoothing the wall. The whole was finished with a white lime wash. Elizabethan plaster used a mixture of sand, slaked lime and animal hair. The new Globe has used a similar historic mixture.

An important difference between the modern and the Elizabethan infill is not visible. To pass modern safety regulations a fire-proof sheet is sealed between the coats of plaster. In laboratory tests it withstood 1,000°c heat for nearly three hours.

As the green oak dries and shrinks, cracks appear, sometimes quite large fissures. In spite of appearances, these do not affect the strength of the building. A timber frame locks into itself as it shifts and settles. Like thatch and plaster, oak breathes. The Globe is a living building which moves with the seasons, never completely still.

far left The skeletal frame, before staves and laths are fixed.
© Peter McCurdy

left Laths and main timber, showing signs of shrinkage.
© Cafferty/Lewis

below A plasterer begins to cover the laths.
© Cafferty/Lewis

SETTING UP THE FRAME

Entrances, exits & galleries

When he visited the Globe in 1599 Thomas Platter made a careful note in his diary of the entry prices. *'Whoever cares to stand below pays only one English penny, but if he wishes to sit he enters by another door, and pays another penny, while if he desires to sit in the most comfortable seats which are cushioned, where he not only sees everything well but can also be seen, then he pays yet another English penny at another door.'* It was cheapest to stand in the yard, only one penny. To do this a 'groundling' came in by one of the Globe's two doors. For a second penny a spectator could sit in the galleries and shelter from the rain. A third penny got the spectator a cushion and a better seat where he could *'be seen'* by the rest of the audience.

Exactly how spectators got into the galleries remains conjectural. External stair towers may have been the standard way of entering the upper levels of an open-air theatre, although the excavations of the Rose so far show no sign of any stair tower foundations. The Swan is known to have had stair towers and Hollar's careful drawing of the second Globe, and his later engraving, clearly show two stair towers breaking the smooth curve of the *'wooden O'*.

The original Globe held around three thousand people. When it burned down in 1613 all three thousand were able to leave safely by *'two small dores'*. Fire regulations are more stringent for modern theatres. In order to get a licence for half that number, the new Globe had to be provided with more and wider exits. There are four exits from the yard and the stair towers have been modified. They have broader stairways and are positioned against bays that let people out at separate points on the outer walls from the yard exits. One and a half thousand people will be able to exit from the theatre in two and half minutes.

Spectators who paid an extra penny for the gallery sat on large

left One of the two stair towers which give access to the galleries. In Elizabethan times the windows would have been shuttered.
© Cafferty/Lewis

above A detail from Wenceslaus Hollar's engraving, the 'Long View of London'. It shows the second Globe and the bear-baiting house, with their names transposed.
By permission of Guildhall Library, Corporation of London.

right Balusters on the middle gallery.
© Cafferty/Lewis

below Oak logs are cut to a length and then cleft repeatedly until they yield three inch (75mm) billets. Each billet is shaved roughly cylindrical. One at a time, the billets are turned on the lathe by means of a leather strap which is suspended from the tip of a long, flexible pole, twisted twice around the billet and attached at the foot to the treadle.

The wood turner Gudrun Leitz treadles to spin the billet while holding a chisel against the revolving wood, cutting it into a perfect round before shaping the patterns of the baluster.
© Derek Harris

steps without backs called *degrees*. Their amply-padded clothing would have meant that this was not too uncomfortable, although there was no legal restriction on how many people could be squeezed in. Two extra pennies gave a seat in a gentleman's room, which was a cushioned section of the gallery nearest to the stage. Prestigious seats were in the Lords' rooms, positioned behind and above the stage. To a modern audience it is surprising to sit behind the actors with restricted viewing but Elizabethan gentry were more than ready to join in the action with comments and witticisms of their own. *'Let that clapper, your tongue, be tossed so high, that all the house may ring of it'*, advises a satirical contemporary book on how young gentlemen should behave at the playhouse.

In the rubble of the Rose excavations, part of a single baluster was discovered. It has been copied as the model for the 315 balusters which run around the middle galleries at the new Globe. Each baluster has been turned, as it would have been in Shakespeare's time, on a pole lathe. These were simple and effective cutting machines, powered by a foot treadle. For hundreds of years turners made them from the natural elements of the countryside: timber, young ash saplings and leather thongs.

ENTRANCES, EXITS & GALLERIES

Thatching the roof

'The house with the thatched roof', as the Swiss visitor Thomas Platter called the first Globe, would have been covered either in straw or water reed. Both were used for thatching in Elizabethan times. In the foundations of the Rose, archæologists found quantities of water reed so the new Globe has been roofed in the same material. Economy and speed were uppermost when the Globe was going up in 1599 so the thatchers probably used local reed which grew plentifully in the Thames valley. For the new Globe, the thatchers had to go further afield to the wetlands of Norfolk to find their water reed.

The art of thatching never died out in the countryside, but London was another matter. After the Great Fire thatching was banned in the capital. The new Globe is the first building in London since 1666 to have a thatched roof, and precautions have been taken to meet stringent modern safety standards. The reeds are treated with a specially formulated chemical which retards burning. Fireboard has been put under the thatch. The third element in the roof protection is a sprinkler system capable of drenching the thatch in minutes. Sparge pipes have been incorporated into the roof ridge, with slim nozzles poking through the ornamental ridge thatching.

left Nozzles of a modern sparge pipe drencher system rise through the traditional thatch patterning on the ridge.
© Tiffany Foster

below The ridge of the Globe is open to the sky before thatching.
© Pentagram Design Limited

above Three views of the roof at different stages of completion: sunlight through the open roof; plaster conceals the fireboard; bundles of reed are carried to the roof.
Top two photographs © Pentagram Design Limited, third photograph by permission of Thatching Advisory Services.

right Starting at the eaves, the thatchers lay the reeds at a steep angle, dress them with a grooved bat, peg them down and finally trim them neatly with shears. In time the reed turns a gentle grey colour.
© Chris Harris, Times Newspapers Limited

The sumptuous stage

left The gilded ribs of the *Heavens* divide the canopy into panels. The painted sky is adorned with sun, moon, signs of the zodiac and a divinely-lit cloud whose central panel hides a trapdoor.
By permission of Gary Swann/Sygma.

below A detail from De Witt's 1596 drawing of the Swan theatre. Two pillars support the stage cover, behind which the musicians' gallery and Lords' rooms can be seen.
By permission of the Rijksuniversiteit, Utrecht.

On the outside an Elizabethan playhouse had plain, limewashed walls. Inside, it was a blaze of colour. As early as 1577, Thomas White describes the playhouses as *'sumptuous'*. When De Witt visited the Swan in 1596 he could hardly believe the stage pillars were wooden because they were *'painted in such excellent imitation of marble that it is able to deceive even the most cunning.'* To Ben Jonson, the first Globe was the *'glory of the Banke'* and John Chamberlain thought the second Globe *'the fairest that ever was in England.'*

Tantalisingly, not a single playhouse stage survives. De Witt's sketch of the Swan stage is the only contemporary view we have and it is based on a lost original. More trustworthy evidence can be deduced from the details of the Fortune playhouse which Peter Street was contracted to build *'like unto the Stadge of the ... Plaiehouse called the Globe ... with a shadowe or cover over the saide stadge.'* A further clue lies in the excavations of the Rose where a drip-line across the yard in front of the stage suggests years of rain running off a thatch cover. The texts of the plays, especially stage directions, give information, such as references

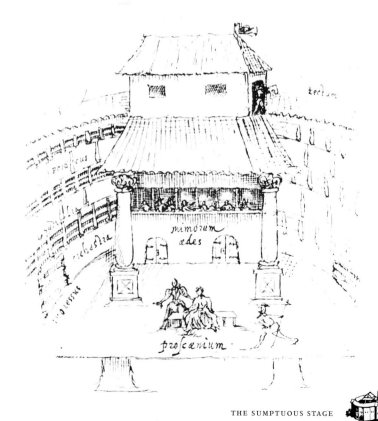

above and opposite A huge stage pillar is slowly lowered into the new Globe.
© Richard Kalina

opposite below The artistic director, Mark Rylance, surveys the carved capital of the stage pillar, safely delivered on site.
© Richard Kalina

to the stage *hangings*. So do period details from surviving wooden buildings: the roof trusses of Middle Temple Hall and Charterhouse in the City, market crosses, guildhalls and Queen Elizabeth's hunting lodge in Epping Forest. For the 1995 and 1996 seasons at the new Globe, temporary stages were constructed so that the practical experience of actors could influence the final design. Because of their unhappiness with the positioning of the pillars, the architects brought them closer together in the final plan and added a 'skirt' or pentice roof which extended the stage cover without adding undue weight. The stage is the most conjectural part of the reconstruction. How authentic is it? It is unlikely we will ever know, but scholars are convinced that the new Globe's stage is how Shakespeare's *could* have looked.

Circumstantial evidence indicates that the Globe had a rectangular stage, five feet high, which projected halfway into the yard. In the *frons scenae* (the back wall) were two side doors, flanking a central opening covered with hangings. Behind the hangings lay the *'discovery'* space where Polonius hid *'behind the arras'* and Paulina *'draws a curtain'* to reveal the statue of Hermione. Above the stage was a balcony for musicians and actors. It could serve as Juliet's balcony or the walls of Flint castle in *Richard II* or Harfleur in *Henry V*.

What astonishes many modern visitors is the size of the great stage cover thrusting out from the *frons scenae*. It is constructed in three parts: a thatched gable, an attached pentice roof covered in lighter oak boards, and a decorated ceiling called the *Heavens*.

The sixteen-ton *Heavens* are supported, at the front, by a single crossbeam resting on two pillars 24 feet high. The main crossbeam is the largest single timber in the building, 41 feet long with a cross-section of 24 x 16 inches. The trees which provided the huge crossbeam and pillars were found in Norfolk and Scotland. First, the trunks for the pillars were shaped to tapered columns. Then, their centres were drilled out by hand using an auger. Boring a small hole down the length of the timbers reduces the risk of splitting and maintains a smooth surface for painting. Peter Street almost certainly did the same with the Fortune's pillars. We know he owned an auger because records show that in 1603 he lent it to the workmen building the Banqueting Hall at Whitehall. In the 1990s, long after such practices had died out, Peter McCurdy had to research and redesign a hand auger to build the new Globe.

To the Elizabethans, the theatre was an image of the universe. Beneath the stage lay Hell, out of which devils or the ghost of Hamlet's father, *'this fellow in the cellarage',* would emerge through a central trap-door. The stage was the earthly region where humans played out their comedies and tragedies. Above hung the canopy of the stage cover, the *Heavens*. The stage area of the new Globe has been painted in earth colours, greys, greens, browns and russet red. The midnight-blue

above Three details of stage decoration: the divinely-lit trapdoor; Mars; the Sun.
top © Pentagram Design Limited
middle and bottom © Richard Kalina

above right A modern craftsman gilds the *Heavens*, delicately applying tissue-thin leaves of gold exactly as an Elizabethan craftsman would have done.
© Richard Kalina

below right Painting the *Heavens*.
© Richard Kalina

above New Zealand's gift to the Globe is a set of four embroidered hangings for the *frons scenae*, designed by Dr Raymond Boyce. One pair shows the heroes of Shakespeare's poem, *Venus and Adonis*, while the other pair have Greek heroes, Atlas and Hercules, whose stories honour the name of the Globe. In classical mythology, Atlas (shown above) bore the globe on his shoulders, except for a brief respite when Hercules relieved him of the burden. The figure of Hercules carrying the globe flew on a flag above the original Globe whenever a play was in progress. Today the new Globe is continuing the tradition.
© Brett Robertson

opposite Rehearsing *Umabatha*, the Zulu *Macbeth*.
© Tristram Kenton

ceiling of the *Heavens* is divided into panels by gilded ribs or *frets* and decorated with stars, sun, moon and the circle of the zodiac. In the centre, a divinely-lit cloud disguises the trap door which can open to lower a god or goddess over the stage. When Lorenzo tells Jessica

*Look how the floor of heaven
Is thick inlaid with patens of bright gold*

the audience at the first Globe would have seen the painted stars on the *Heavens*' ceiling. Hamlet was looking up at the gilded *frets* when he addressed Rosencrantz and Guildenstern.

... look you, this brave o'erhanging firmament, this majestical roof fretted with golden fire.

Although it is hard to believe, all the stage is made of oak. As in Elizabethan times, skilled painters splotched, dabbed, veined and burnished to create the illusion of stone, marble and semi-precious minerals. Tudor decoration was studied on walls and hangings, on tapestries and tombs, on bedposts and ships' figure-heads, in drawings and prints of ceremonial presentations, to find models for the decorations on the *frons scenae*. Above the balcony, seven planetary deities, believed to influence earthly events, are painted in *grisaille*. At either end stand Mercury and Apollo, the Gods of eloquent speech, while the bare-breasted Muses of Tragedy and Comedy look benignly down from the balcony. And on the front of the *Heavens*, between decorations of Elizabethan strapwork, the winged figure of Fame blows her trumpet.

Recent scholarship has made a surprising new discovery. The first Globe's stage faced 48 degrees east of north, placing it in continual shadow. Winter and summer, the players acted under cover and out of the light. This may have been to conserve their valuable costumes. The rich dyes and fabrics, set against the brilliantly painted stage, were part of the dazzling appearance of the interior of the Globe which so impressed the Elizabethans.

The reconstruction of the Globe is as faithful to the original as scholarship and craftsmanship can make it, but no one believes it is possible to turn back the clock completely. Nor would we want to. Elizabethan audiences accepted conditions which would discomfort us today. They rarely washed, themselves or their clothes. They packed into playhouses so closely that Thomas Dekker describes the theatres steaming with boiling, red-faced 'Stinkards'. '*Their houses smoakt every after noone with Stinkards who were so glewed together in crowdes with the Steames of strong breath, that when they came foorth, their faces lookt as if they had beene per boylde*' (par-boiled). They ate and drank throughout performances, interrupted at will, broke into fights and hissed and clapped the action. Reports probably highlight the more rumbustious incidents. Audiences must have felt safe since the playhouses attracted a range of society. All sorts of people came to the Globe, wrote John Chamberlain in 1624, '*old and young, rich and poor, master and servants, papists and puritans.*'

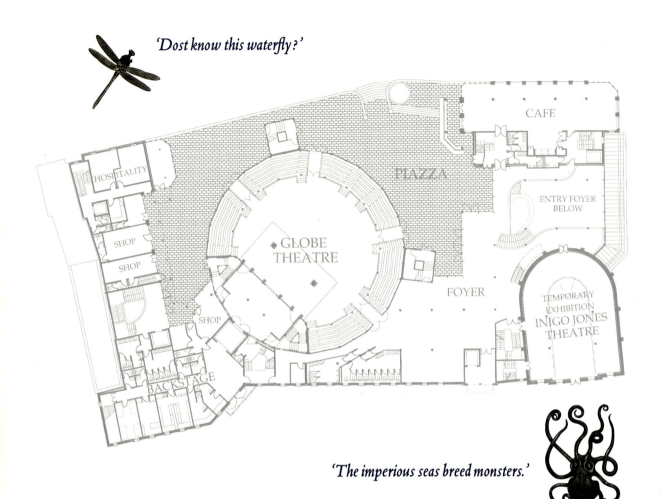

'Dost know this waterfly?'

'The imperious seas breed monsters.'

The Globe Centre

'The Globe is a simple white plastered building, tiny by modern standards', wrote the architect Theo Crosby, 'but it carries an astonishing authority ... Everyone knows about and carries a mental image of it ... The buildings around, therefore, are doubly important: they have to sustain the illusion of the physical importance of the Globe, and provide a complex visual background to counter its formal simplicity.'

When complete, the Globe Centre will contain an exhibition, a library and an education and research centre, as well as shops, a cafeteria and a restaurant. Theo Crosby planned the buildings in a variety of popular styles, giving the simple Globe a setting which displays its difference and its eminence.

Throughout the year, Shakespeare's company played at the Globe. Audiences must have been willing to brave all weathers in Elizabethan times. James Burbage always intended the company to move indoors for the winter, and in 1608 his sons retrieved the Blackfriars, the winter playhouse which he had expensively fitted out in 1596. From then on, the company played at the Globe in the summer and at the smaller Blackfriars in the winter.

To reconstruct the original playing conditions, the ISGC

left Plan of the piazza level of the Globe Centre.
below Architect's drawing of the north side of the Centre facing the Thames.
Photographs, plan and drawing by permission of Pentagram Design Limited.

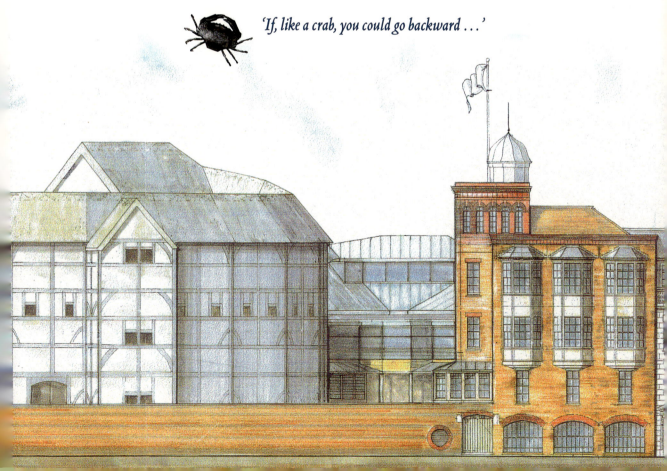

'If, like a crab, you could go backward ...'

opposite Gates designed by Richard Quinnell close the perimeter wall. They are decorated with small animals, birds, insects and plants, forged by metal workers from around the world. Each object illustrates a quotation from Shakespeare.
© Pentagram Design limited

right Two views of the Inigo Jones theatre, the tiled roof and the neo-classical facade.
© Pentagram Design Limited

thought it important to have both kinds of theatre, indoor and outdoor. Even less is known about the design of the Blackfriars than of the Globe, so it was decided to use a set of plans discovered in Worcester College, Oxford, as recently as 1969. These show Inigo Jones' designs for an indoor playhouse that imitated the Blackfriars. There is no evidence that the designs were realised in the seventeenth century, but, built of small hand-made bricks in the Tudor style and with a neo-classical pediment, the Inigo Jones Theatre now takes its place in the 1990s Globe Centre.

Performances in the twin theatres will realise Sam Wanamaker's dream, a fit memorial to the playwright of whom his friend Ben Jonson wrote

'Thou art a Monument without a tomb,
And art alive still, while thy Book doth live.'

Theo Crosby
1925–1994

Theo Crosby, designer, architect, writer, lecturer and founder-member of the Pentagram Design Group, was the architect of the Globe project for twenty-five years. A South African by birth, he studied at Witwatersrand University and, after war service in Italy, came to England in the early fifties, a dissident from apartheid. Like most of the Bauhaus-trained generation of architects he started as a modernist, but in the sixties he began to question the ideology of the vast post-war building programmes. He was a member of the Preservation Policy Group which established basic conservation studies and essential legislation.

He met Sam Wanamaker at a time when he was arguing that, rather than starting with a clean sweep of existing buildings, it was important for community life to conserve the environment and mix old and new architecture. The idea of rebuilding Shakespeare's Globe fitted precisely his vision of what made city life natural, popular and richly interesting. He was present at one of Sam's early presentations and offered to help, thinking in terms of designing a brochure. Instead he found himself signing on for life. *'I started by putting a toe in the water and the next thing I knew – I was swimming.'* He shared Sam's vision of the new Globe taking its place within a revitalised Southwark, relating to the community who live beside it, offering educational opportunities to all who work in it and drawing visitors like a magnet.

Photograph by permission of Pentagram Design Limited